Orchids & Roses
❧ COLORING BOOK ❧

Exotic orchids used to be so expensive that only the very wealthy grew them or purchased them. Roses of all sorts, on the other hand, have long been tended by rich and poor alike. Today, both species of blooms are the favorites of countless gardeners.

The botanical illustrations included in this coloring book are held in the collection of the Royal Botanic Garden Edinburgh. Whether you choose to color in keeping with the originals—shown on the inside covers—or create your own orchid and rose "varieties" using new hues, each page is blank on the back and suitable for framing. We've even included a page on which you can draw and color an orchid or rose to be named after you—in Latin, of course.

Royal
Botanic Garden
Edinburgh

Pomegranate

The line drawings presented here are based on works in the collection of the Royal Botanic Garden Edinburgh:

1. John Nugent Fitch (English, 1840–1927). *Lælia præstans* from *The Orchid Album* (London, 1892), vol. 10, plate 433.

2. John Lindley (English, 1799–1865). *Rosa clare* from *Edwards's Botanical Register* (London, 1831), vol. 17, plate 1438.

3. John Nugent Fitch (English, 1840–1927). *Cymbidium pendulum* from *The Orchid Album* (London, 1892), vol. 10, plate 437.

4. Henry Charles Andrews (English, fl. 1794–1830). *Rosa semperflorens* from *Roses, or, A Monograph of the Genus* Rosa (London, 1828), vol. 2, plate 72.

5. John Nugent Fitch (English, 1840–1927). *Chysis bractescens* from *The Orchid Album* (London, 1892), vol. 10, plate 446.

6. John Lindley (English, 1799–1865). *Rosa multiflora* var. *platyphylla* from *Edwards's Botanical Register* (London, 1830), vol. 16, plate 1372.

7. John Nugent Fitch (English, 1840–1927). *Calanthe vestita Oweniana* from *The Orchid Album* (London, 1892), vol. 10, plate 464.

8. Joseph Dalton Hooker (English, 1817–1911). *Rosa microphylla* from *Curtis's Botanical Magazine: Plants of the Royal Gardens of Kew* (London, 1881), vol. 37, plate 6548.

9. John Nugent Fitch (English, 1840–1927). *Cattleya Dowiana aurea Statteriana* from *The Orchid Album* (London, 1892), vol. 10, plate 468.

10. Mary Lawrance (English, fl. 1790–1831). *Rosa centifolia* from A *Collection of Roses from Nature* (London, 1799), plate 46.

11. John Nugent Fitch (English, 1840–1927). *Cymbidium lowianum* from *The Orchid Album* (London, 1892), vol. 10, plate 471.

12. Unknown artist. *Rosa moyesii* from *The Garden*, vol. 80, no. 2344, (London, 1916), plate 1505.

13. John Nugent Fitch (English, 1840–1927). *Odontoglossum prionopetalum* from *The Orchid Album* (London, 1892), vol. 10, plate 474.

14. Mary Lawrance (English, fl. 1790–1831). *Rosa lutea ß bicolor* from *A Collection of Roses from Nature* (London, 1799), plate 6.

15. John Nugent Fitch (English, 1840–1927). *Phajus Cooksonii* from *The Orchid Album* (London, 1892), vol. 10, plate 478.

16. Henry Charles Andrews (English, fl. 1794–1830). *Rosa inermis* from *Roses, or, A Monograph of the Genus* Rosa (London, 1828), vol. 2, plate 88.

17. Gertrude Hamilton. *Chysis lævis* from *The Orchid Album* (London, 1896), vol. 11, plate 482.

18. Henry Charles Andrews (English, fl. 1794–1830). *Rosa gallica variegata* from *Roses, or, A Monograph of the Genus* Rosa (London, 1805), vol. 1.

19. John Nugent Fitch (English, 1840–1927). *Sophronitis grandiflora* from *The Orchid Album* (London, 1896), vol. 11, plate 504.

20. John Sims (English, 1749–1831). *Rosa gallica (ß versicolor)* from *Curtis's Botanical Magazine: Flower-Garden Displayed* (London, 1816), vol. 43, plate 1794.

21. John Nugent Fitch (English, 1840–1927). *Vanda cœrulea* from *The Orchid Album* (London, 1896), vol. 11, plate 517.

22. Unknown artist. *Rosa thé Isabella Gray* from *Flore des Serres et des Jardins de L'Europe* (1857), tome 12, page 75.

· ·

Pomegranate Communications, Inc.
19018 NE Portal Way, Portland OR 97230
800 227 1428   www.pomegranate.com

Pomegranate's mission is to invigorate, illuminate, and inspire through art.

© 2015 Royal Botanic Garden Edinburgh
Color images © 2015 Royal Botanic Garden Edinburgh
Line drawings © Pomegranate Communications, Inc.

Item No. CB166

Designed by Carey Hall

Printed in Korea

25 24 23 22 21 20 19 18 17 16   11 10 9 8 7 6 5 4 3 2

Distributed by Pomegranate Europe Ltd.
'number three', Siskin Drive, Middlemarch Business Park
Coventry CV3 4FJ, UK
sales@pomeurope.co.uk

1. *Lælia præstans*

2. Rosa clare

3. *Cymbidium pendulum*

4. Rosa semperflorens

5. *Chysis bractescens*

6. *Rosa multiflora* var. *platyphylla*

7. *Calanthe vestita Oweniana*

8. *Rosa microphylla*

9. *Cattleya Dowiana aurea Statteriana*

10. *Rosa centifolia*

11. *Cymbidium lowianum*

12. *Rosa moyesii*

13. *Odontoglossum prionopetalum*

14. *Rosa lutea ß bicolor*

15. *Phajus Cooksonii*

16. *Rosa inermis*

17. *Chysis lævis*

18. *Rosa gallica variegata*

19. *Sophronitis grandiflora*

20. *Rosa gallica* (ß *versicolor*)

21. Vanda cœrulea

22. *Rosa thé Isabella Gray*

Draw and color your own picture here!